BEYOND

BREAKING

EVEN

YOUR TOOLBOX TO BUILDING EXPONENTIAL PROFITS

Catherine M. White

Accelerated Results 365

I dedicate this book to Sarah and Bruno Balogh for giving me the opportunity to help you in the remodeling of your home that inspired the writing and theme of this book.

Praise for Beyond Breaking Even & The P.O.W.E.R.R.™ System

Catherine White has given a gift to every business owner who reads this book. Well laid out content with engaging questions and analogies. This book helps you map out the blueprint for your business from start to finish and everything in between. From mindset, market analysis, communication skills and more, your business will grow using the tools she provides.

-Rae Ann Hall, Founder, Hall Insurance Agency

Beyond Breaking Even is a perfect book for anyone who is new to business or is hoping to grow their existing business. In the language of construction, it is a perfect blueprint to create a successful, cash positive business. From planning to implementation, Beyond Breaking Even gives you the tools you need to form a great foundation, to create a business model that will weather the storms. I highly recommend this to small business owners everywhere.

-Jake Hanes, CPA; Author *"7 Strategies of Highly Successful Business Owners"*

With simple, effective tips, Beyond Breaking Even, is a must read for anyone starting a business or actively growing one. Think of it as your flight checklist to make sure you get everything right before takeoff.

-Taylor Clouse, Bookkeeper and Profit Advisor, Next Level Books, LLC

Thrilled to have found Beyond Breaking Even, a great resource for any new or growing business. The clear, concise, step-by-step process is easy to understand for anybody with a small business. Covering everything from starting a business, overcoming obstacles, to expanding make this a great resource to keep close on hand as your guidebook to success.

-Karen Rae, Founder, Fave Lifestyles

Catherine is smart and compassionate. She will guide you with expertise and strength. Beyond Breaking Even is creative and practical - this information will propel you toward success! Catherine has the business growth strategies you need. Do yourself a favor, connect with Catherine today!

-Dani Green, Creator, Higher Path Healing

After reading Beyond Breaking Even, I was sure that we are facing a great work that guides anyone who wants to start a business to be successful. All the phases you have to go through and step by step to achieve success. Everyone who wants to start a new business should read this book first. Without Courage and Commitment, you never start anything and without Consistency and Confidence, it never ends. Thank you, Catherine for showing me the way by aiming to the Stars with the P.O.W.E.R.R. System and the Accelerated Results 365 that I highly recommend.

-Paulo Pereira, Networking Modern Entrepreneur

Beyond Breaking Even by Catherine White is a book anyone in business for themselves will gain tremendous insight to start or build their business. Catherine's analogy of building a business like you would build a new home makes it relatable and fun. Her questions, insights, and encouragement moves you into new understanding that will create the change you may be looking for. I highly recommend Beyond Breaking Even. You will come away with a success outlook in moving your business to a new level.

-Coralee Kulman, Come Alive Coach

In Beyond Breaking Even, Catherine M. White takes us through the building and nurturing process of a successful business. She troubleshoots potential pitfalls, points out resources, and hands over the right tool for the job each step of the way. This is an impressive accomplishment.

-Arthur Longworth, Owner, Singing Heart Ranch; Award Winning Author

Catherine's go-get-'em attitude and personal attention elevate her insights and smart systems approach to equal massive benefits for every business owner who knows her. Friendly and outgoing, Catherine's approach is an easily understood framework for success. What I truly appreciate about Catherine is her ability to connect: people, ideas, intentions, and energies to the benefit of all who know her.

-Jeremy Tank, Founder, Think Tank Creative

Catherine is beyond amazing! I was struggling at generating business in my new chosen career and she helped me to see my roadblocks...within 2 weeks I had more referrals than ever and had tripled my business.

-Kira Truett, Mortgage Advisor, CrossCountry Mortgage, LLC

Catherine is an extraordinary person who quickly empathizes with her clients and helps them achieve whatever goals they set. I recommend to those who want to be successful but are stuck to contact her and let her work with you to relieve those symptoms, and help you get on the road to success.

- Megan Martineau, Founder, Honeybee Photography

P.O.W.E.R.R. is a well thought out innovative system to help anyone in any industry set the right types of goals and achieve them. Catherine is a wonderful accountability partner who pushes you to think outside the box for solutions.

-Amber Chang, Co-founder, bulldog & burbon

Catherine M. White is an epitome of the powerhouse. She has got profound sense and understanding, which enables us to get glued to what she is saying. She is a great speaker who knows to deliver the content according to who the recipient is and what level of understanding he/she has about life. Catherine's session on "Break Your Box with P.O.W.E.R.R." was revolutionary.

-Ryan Timothy Rishab, Budding Entrepreneur

FOREWORD

I met Catherine from the back of an Uber while she was driving me home from Sea-Tac airport. Because I travel a great deal for business, I've ridden in the back of many Ubers and met countless drivers. What struck me about Catherine, and what led to our friendship, was her genuine curiosity in my professional endeavors and her willingness to share her own compelling vision for a life beyond Uber.

After reading her book, *Beyond Breaking Even*, I experienced two distinct feelings: first, I was proud of her for producing such a valuable publication; second, I was annoyed that I had not read her book prior to starting two companies of my own.

There is no shame in not knowing how to run a small business, let alone, how to make it profitable, when you are first starting out. It would be a shame, though, not to embrace simple solutions, like those Catherine is offering in this book, when your business is only breaking even.

I could rhapsodize about Catherine's deep knowledge of her topic, the extensive research she did to create all the helpful exercises, tips, and tools provided herein. Instead, I'm going to cite a quote: "Only fools rush in."

This saying, which dates back to an 18th Century poem by Alexander Pope, was popularized by an Elvis Presley song of the same name. But the saying applies as much to relationships as it does to business. And what Catherine makes explicit in Beyond Breaking Even is the need for preparation, for planning with intention and methodical execution of those plans.

Don't be a fool. Read the rest of this book. And, more importantly, embrace the knowledge that will lead you beyond breaking even to a winning path of profitability.

Brent Friedman
Hollywood Writer & Producer
and Entrepreneur

TABLE OF CONTENTS

INTRODUCTION

You are reading this book because you want to make money in your business – lots of money, right?! While many business owners focus on revenue, there is one thing more important than generating revenue – that is making a profit. You can make a lot of money and never become wealthy. And you can produce high revenues in your business and never make a profit.

Do you recall when you worked for someone else? Did you ever find yourself saying, "My paycheck is gone before it even hits the bank?" These are common words of someone who is working a job and living paycheck to paycheck – your bills are the same every month so you know exactly how much of your income will be spent on your monthly expenses. If all your bills are paid and you have nothing left over, you have broken even. If you still have a portion of your paycheck remaining after all expenses are paid, you have a surplus – in business, when all expenses are paid and there is money left over, we call it a profit. If your expenses are greater than your income and you have bills left unpaid or you are using credit cards and loans to pay what is left, you have a deficit or a loss.

According to The National Federation of Independent Business (NFIB), less than 40 percent of small businesses make a profit over the lifetime of the business, 30 percent break even, and another 30 percent lose money.[1] If less than half of businesses are making a profit, how are they still in business? Well, they float by, with many sinking further and further into debt until they break and close.

Whether you are just starting out or you have been in business for several years, you will fall among one of these statistics.

Where does your business currently land? Whichever of these three categories you fit into, this book is for you.

If you are losing money – you are on the verge of folding and better do something FAST before it is too late!

If you are already at the breakeven point, meaning the revenue coming in equals your expenses going out, it will take just some minor tweaks to move one way the other; it could be an unexpected expense or emergency that increases your outgoing funds or a slight to large drop in sales that hinders your ability to cover your expenditures and knocks you backward into the "losing money" category. On the other hand, you can make a small adjustment to bump up your sales and place you into the "making a profit" group. Chances are, if you keep doing whatever you are doing now, you will likely slide backward. It takes little effort to lose money and a lot more to make it.

Perhaps you are already making a profit. Since a

profit can be as little as being one dollar above your expenses, profits alone are not a good measuring tool in determining the success of your business. You need to be looking at your profit margin which is the gap between your expenses and your revenue. The higher the margin, the greater the chance your business will withstand changes in the economy.

The beauty of reaching profitability is that it becomes easier to duplicate what works to exponentially grow your profits. However, to consistently increase your profits at an exponential rate, it will require consistent change and progression because the market is forever evolving. Never during the life of your business will you reach a time when you can stop and just glide along and produce a continuous profit without effort. Just like with driving a car, once you take your foot off the accelerator, you will begin to slow down and eventually come to a stop.

We have found there are three core obstacles that hinder the growth, profitability, and sustainability of a business: low employee morale, lack of clarity with organizational goals and high market competition.

1. Low employee morale.

The growth of your company weighs heavily on your employees; if they are not actively engaged and highly producing, it is costing you money. You will spend more time on mundane tasks and less time on revenue generating activities. You in turn, throw away money by paying employees who are not producing to their potential. They eventually become complacent and move on to brighter and greener pastures, increasing your turnover rates which then creates greater hiring and training costs. (This is true for any size of team, including the one that is made up of only *you*.)

2. **Lack of clarity.**

   Your company's mission statement is the backbone of your organization; it is what guides you and your employees. When your team is unclear about your mission, everyone ends up doing their own thing and no one focuses on the company's mission; therefore, organizational goals are left unmet.

3. **High market competition.**

   In nearly every industry, there is a lot of competition and many companies are clueless in how to stand out and be seen above others. If you're like other companies in the industry, you're not just dealing with spinning your wheels to achieve your goals, you're wondering how to stay ahead, trying to make sure not to lose accounts or your edge in the marketplace. Not knowing how to gain an advantage among your competition can quickly put your profits in a downward spiral.

If you are struggling in one or more of these areas, it is not your fault. Business owners often don't know how to handle these three problem areas because they've never been taught how to effectively solve these issues; they're just expected to "figure it out" without the proper training and then it gets swept under the carpet because no one wants to deal with it or admit it's a problem. This is where Accelerated Results 365 comes in to act as your guide so you can be the hero among your team and in your community.

In the following pages, you will find several tools to use to run a business that performs highly in each of these areas and be on the path to building exponential profits.

Before we begin, imagine you have been renting a condo for ten years and you are sick and tired of the many restrictions placed on you by the HOA. When you receive a notice that your rent is increasing due to a rise in HOA fees, you decide you are done with renting. You think to yourself, "Why should I pay another penny to support something I hate?!"

You decide it's time to stop renting and buy but you feel the housing market is overinflated and you can build yourself a home for a fraction of the cost. You get in your car and drive down to the nearest building supply store. Once inside, you grab a shopping cart and walk down the isles one at a time, picking out tools along the way and placing them in your cart. Next, you head over to the lumber area and pick out several planks of wood then proceed to the checkout line. When the cashier rings up your order and gives you the total you begin to panic because you are not sure there's enough money in your bank account to cover the expense. You silently ask yourself which tools you can do without and remove the two most expensive ones to ensure you don't overdraw the account.

When you return home, you sit down at your laptop and search YouTube for a video on "How to build my first home".

How many things can you find wrong with this scenario? Here are the four most obvious errors:

1. You have never built a house before; therefore, you are lacking knowledge and experience.

2. You do not have a plan or blueprint for building the house.

3. You do not have a list of tools and materials needed.

4. You have not run a cost analysis and budgeted your expenses.

While most people would not build a house this way, many do build a business like this. They decide they are sick and tired of working for someone else, so they jump into a business without the proper knowledge, tools, and plan. They then rely on the internet to tell them how to run their business. The problem is there is a lot of confusing and inaccurate information and an overabundance of people claiming they can show you how to make a quick and easy six to seven figure income to lure you into paying for overpriced programs that teach you little to nothing about growing your business.

Just as with building a house, there are multiple steps in building a business and generating exponential profits. I break it down into four phases:

1. Plan
2. Build
3. Grow
4. Expand

Because many small businesses are created haphazardly, missing important steps in the process, I encourage you to read through each section, whether you are just starting out or you have owned your business for several years. In order to become exponentially profitable, you first need to make sure you have a solid framework in place to sustain massive growth. After all, you wouldn't put a roof on a house that had a sinking foundation and caved in walls, would you?

PHASE ONE

PLAN

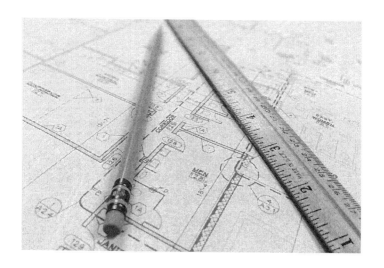

Measure twice, cut once.

Russian proverb

Chapter
1

FAST FORWARD

One of the most common challenges homeowners face is that they begin the construction process before they have a clear picture of what they want their house to look like and then they spend a lot of time and money on redrawing blueprints, tearing out unwanted structures and revising designs. It's important to take time to research and visualize your needs and desires.

> If a client takes the time to look forward and picture what their home might look like it will help the decision-making process for what character, design elements and features are included. You will save time and money with proper planning of your project.
>
> (Brad Sturman, Founder, Sturman Architects, Inc.)

This is just as important to do with your business before you start new or make changes to an existing company. Make sure you take time to visualize what you want your business to look like and what you wish to get out of owning it.

Fast forward and imagine yourself 10 years down the road and consider what your company will look like. How big will your business be? Will you run it by yourself or will you bring on a partner? Will you hire or bring on more employees? Will you have a storefront in multiple locations? Will you stay national or expand into multiple parts of the world?

What will your personal life be like? Do you currently have, or will you have, a spouse and children? How much time will you spend in your business versus with your family or as personal time? Where will you live? What kind of home will you live in? What kind of car with you drive? How will you dress? How will you behave?

Continue to expand on these questions and create a detailed visualization of your business and your personal life.

Building Exponential Profits
Tool # 1 – The Journal

A journal is not typically considered a tool used for building a house but think of the benefit of keeping a journal during the construction process. If you were building or remodeling your home, a journal is a place where you could take notes as you study homes and choose what features and designs you want to incorporate into your house. You could also write about your feelings as you go through the process, so you have something to look back on and reminisce over after the house is complete. This will be a good reminder of the challenges and the joys you experienced and may strengthen your appreciation for what you built.

As you visualize your dreams for your business, keep a journal of your goals, needs and desires. Document the obstacles you face and your achievements. This will be a great resource to have and look back through any time you question your reason for doing what you do, when you feel like you want to quit, and to also compare what you end up building versus how you envisioned it – into something even better.

Chapter
2

IS BUILDING RIGHT FOR YOU?

Just as there are multiple ways in which you can
obtain home ownership (purchase with a
mortgage, cash, or a combination of both; build it
yourself; hire professionals to build it; or wait for a
possible inheritance), there are many ways to
become a business owner. It is up to you to decide
the best route of ownership for you. Will you start
your own business from the ground up, buy an
existing company, purchase a franchise
opportunity, or join a direct sales company (also
known as network marketing)? There are pros and
cons that come with each option. Be sure to take
the time to learn about each and choose the best
one for you.

Many people make the mistake of thinking that
starting their own business is their ticket to
freedom and wealth. If you are like most business
owners, you want to have control of your time,
your money, and ultimately your life by doing
something that you are passionate about and truly
enjoy doing. Although ownership has many great
benefits, it takes a lot of work and time to build a
business that many people are not properly
prepared for.

Often, when I first meet someone who asks me
what I do for a living and I tell them I own a

business, they express envy. One of my favorite responses is, "You are so lucky that you can take a vacation whenever you want and you don't have to wait for approval from anyone." They then go on to tell me how disgruntled they are about the vacation requests they had submitted to their employer that were denied due to a staff shortage or important projects with deadlines.

I chuckle to myself as I listen and then I explain that most business owners, at least in the first few years from startup, do not take vacations, or at least not paid ones like you may get from an employer. Until you have built a self-sustaining business, when you take a vacation, the money stops. It takes a lot of work and planning to build your business to a point that you are generating an income while you're not working and to ensure the business continues to run smoothly while you are away.

Owning a business is not for everyone. Many people have the misconception that when they own their own business they will have time and money to do what they want when they want, and when they find that it takes more time and effort to build their own business than what they were spending at their full-time job, they quit. Statistics show that only 50 percent of businesses survive the first five years and 30 percent make it beyond 10.[2]

Owning a business comes with a trade-off. In the

early stages of your business, you will put in a lot of work and many hours. If you have a viable business and you build it correctly, you can grow it to a level that allows you to have time freedom and the money you desire – it won't happen overnight. As you become more and more successful, it will appear to others as though your success came quickly and easily because most won't see the hard work that went into your accomplishments. You may know some business owners yourself that you envy because it seems they hit the jackpot of business success. Chances are, they too persevered through big challenges to get to where they are.

> I'm the best twenty-year, overnight success you've ever met.
>
> (John Chen, Founder, Geoteaming – listen at www.rockstarachievers.com)

Here are some questions to ask yourself to determine if you are ready to own a business:

- Am I a self-starter?

- Am I driven and willing to challenge myself?

- Am I willing to take risks, fail, and keep trying after each failure?

- Am I innovative and able to come up with new and fresh ideas?

- Am I a leader?

- Am I considered an influencer within my community, at work, and among friends and family?

- Am I productive when I work alone?

- Am I a team builder and able to work effectively with others?

- Am I willing to ask for feedback from others?

- Am I willing to listen to, consider, and implement the ideas of others?

- Am I willing to step outside of my comfort zone and do things that others won't do?

- Am I able to turn a passion or hobby into a profitable venture?

- Am I willing to work without pay and benefits?

- Am I willing to work overtime?

- Am I willing to invest time and money in personal growth, even when on a tight budget?

- Am I willing to invest time and money in the development of my business at all stages of the business?

- Am I committed to doing whatever it takes (within legal, ethical and moral boundaries) to be successful?

If you answered "yes" to all these questions, you are ready!

If you answered "no" to any of these, ownership may not be right for you at this time. The more of these questions you can honestly say "yes" to, the higher chance you have at generating exponential profits in your business.

Building Exponential Profits
Tool # 2 – The Carpenter Pencil

A carpenter pencil is a special pencil designed with multiple purposes not performed by a standard writing pencil. Rather than a round shape, it is rectangular with four corners and four flat sides. Because of its form, it is easier to grip and can be set down without the worry of it rolling away. The shape also provides the ability to draw thick or thin lines simply by rotating the pencil.

This pencil is not right for use in every circumstance. For example, it would not be a good choice to use in writing an essay. But it is a great option for use in carpentry or construction work that does not require a lot of writing.

Like this pencil, not every person is designed for every circumstance; not everyone makes a good business owner. Some are great at being an employee and become very successful managers, executives, and CEOs. Choose the path that excites you, pushes you, and fulfills you.

Whatever route you choose, become the best at what you do, strive for continual growth, **stand out**, and make a difference.

Chapter
3

DRAWING THE BLUEPRINTS

When you build a house, there is a lot of prep-work that goes into getting started, long before the building process begins. The first thing you will need is a plan which includes deciding the kind of house you want, where you want to live, how many bedrooms and bathrooms you will have, what other types of spaces you want to include, and the size and design of each. You will then have a blueprint drawn up that shows the dimensions and layout of each area.

Next, you will want to put together a cost analysis of building your home so you can create a budget of expenses. This will include the cost of materials and any labor you will hire for the planning, building, and designing of the house. If you find the budget shows you are above your financial ability to cover the necessary expenses, you can adjust your plan.

In business, your blueprint is your business plan. There are several components of creating a business plan. After you have done your prep-work, put your plan in writing. Having a written plan will provide you with direction and keep you focused on your goals; this will help you overcome both expected and unexpected challenges. It's not a matter of "if" you will face obstacles but rather "when" you will.

Follow this process for developing your written plan.

1. **Determine whether you will sell a product or service and what it will be.**

   If you already have a business, you may consider adding additional products or services to boost your revenue (we will cover this in more detail during the expansion phase).

   Here is an exercise for brainstorming ideas for your offer:

   - Make a list of your hobbies, things you enjoy doing that you are good at, talents, special skills, and things that move, motivate, and inspire you.

   - Make a list of items you can create, build, or invent.

   - Make a list of products that you enjoy using and that others enjoy and use often.

   - Make a list of things you like to share with, do for, and teach others.

   - Review your list and circle everything that you believe is sellable.

- Pick the top two to five ideas that you would most enjoy selling.

- Ask yourself, "How will each of these products or services make my potential customer's life easier and better?" In other words, why would someone buy it from you? (Your ability to answer this question will help determine whether or not you have a viable offer.)

- Ask yourself, "Am I passionate enough about this to eat, sleep and drink it?" You are going to be spending so much time on building your business and become so adsorbed in it that it will *feel* like you are eating, sleeping, and drinking it.

- Ask yourself, "Am I passionate enough about it to do it without pay?" When you are new in business, or offering a new addon product or service, it will take time to get it out into the marketplace to be seen. We also live in a time when people are looking for "freemiums" – products or services you offer at no charge with an option for the customer to upgrade for a fee. For instance, many of the apps you download to your smartphone use a freemium model, allowing you access to limited features at no cost; if you want to use the advanced features, you will have to pay.

What this means for you is you will likely be offering your product or service for a time for free or low cost to generate a following that will lead to potential clients.

- Ask yourself, "Am I committed enough to keep pushing forward when I hit roadblocks and feel like a failure?" Running a business has many challenges and if you are not passionate and committed enough about what you do, you will quickly become discouraged and want to give up. This is one reason why so many businesses fail within the first five years.

2. Study and get to know your market.

Many people make the mistake of starting and running a business based off what they want rather than what the market wants and then wonder why their business is not growing. Remember, it is not about you, it is about your prospective customers. Do some research to find out if the product or service you will sell, or are currently selling, is something people will want or need to buy. If you do your research before you jump into the market you will save yourself a lot of frustration, headache, and money.

Here is a simple process for doing a market analysis to determine whether you have a marketable product or service before you begin your business or if you are adding on to what you currently offer. (As you do this, keep in mind, you are only gathering information at this point. You are NOT selling anything.):

- Prepare a survey of questions you want to find answers to, such as, would they have a need or want for it? If given the opportunity would they buy it? How much would they be willing to pay for it? Would they buy if for themselves, for someone else or for a gift? Who else do they know that might have an interest in it?

  You can create free online surveys to send out to your connections via email, text, and social media (these surveys are another example of freemium services – you can use select features for free and pay for the use of additional options).

  To find these free online surveys and other free resources, check out my resources page at:
  www.beyondbreakingeven.com/resources.

- Talk to your friends, family, co-workers, and other acquaintances and ask for their opinion about what you have to offer. Most people love to give advice. Tell them your ideas and ask if they would buy or use what you plan to sell.

- Get connected with other professionals and business owners. Observe what they are doing, what they sell, and how they market it.

- Search the internet and local business listings to see how many companies offer what you have or something similar. Consider whether the market is already saturated of if there's room for another company to profitably offer it.

- Document who you speak with, their answers, and their demographics, such as age, income range, gender, location, and interests. (People tend to be sensitive about this kind of information so you may want to observe and make your best guess rather than ask.) You will notice trends around the types of people and their behaviors who are interested in what you sell; this will help you define your target market.

- At the end of your conversations ask permission to reach out to them and add them to an email list so you can send them more information. They may become either clients or great referral sources.

Remember that you are simply looking for feedback and building connections. In general, people do not like to be sold to; the minute they feel like they are being sold to, you are probably going to get resistance from them. If you are not careful, you can damage the relationship – this is not a good way to build a business.

When you ask permission, many people will be open to you contacting them at a later date because they are curious and want to know whether or not you followed through and if you were successful. When they see that you commit and do as you say, it builds credibility and trust – and makes for a great start to a prospect list.

3. **Run a cost analysis, prepare a budget, and determine how you will fund your venture or expansion.**

Decide on how you will finance the cost of doing business while you build, including any loss of income from leaving your current employment. Do you have investment assets you can put toward your business (before withdrawing from any investments, specifically funds designated for retirement, consult a financial advisor to assess the long-term results and tax consequences of liquidating your assets)? Will you continue working another job or side business? Do you have friends or family that will loan you the money? Will you obtain financing through credit cards or loans?

Before you choose which route you go for funding your business, be sure to consult a professional such as a financial advisor, CPA, and business consultant and consider both the short and long-term ramifications.

4. **Choose a business name to represent your company and what you offer.**

The name you choose for your business will have an impact on the type of customers you attract. Here are some steps for choosing an appropriate name. Make a list of words and phrases that come to mind as you go through each of these.

- Select something short and easy to remember. Two to three-words is a good length.

- Be unique. You want something that will set you apart from other similar businesses.

- Make it catchy and memorable so that when potential customers hear the name it sparks an interest or curiosity for them to want to know more about what you do.

- Consider the feelings and emotions you want to invoke with your potential clients. What energy do you want to emanate? For example, if you offer spiritual healing or massage therapy you might want to create a subdued energy that evokes peace and relaxation. If you offer physical fitness training, you will likely want a name that represents high energy and provokes movement.

- Think of your personal values and what principles you want to portray through your business.

- Determine the level of quality you want to offer. Are you providing something of lower quality, such as discount items to people on a tight budget or are you selling a high-end product to people who are willing to pay premium prices?

- Decide what age group and gender you plan to sell to. This too will make a difference in the name you choose. You want something that will appeal to that specific demographic market.

- Take the list that you have created and brainstorm synonyms and other similar words that are less commonly used. A thesaurus is very handy for this exercise and you can find one online at www.thesaurus.com.

- From your list, create word combinations of two to three words that could be possible business names.

- Conduct an online keyword search to see how frequently those words or phrases are searched for. This is good information for when you are ready to create an online presence and you want to know if people are searching for what you are offering.

  You can use Google and other search engines to do this by typing the phrase into the search bar. As you begin typing, a drop-down list will pop up showing that phrase as well as other similar ones; the ones that show are highly searched phrases.

  There are also sites that are specifically designed for keyword searches, such as www.keywordspy.com, that collect data and will tell you the number of times those words and phrases have been searched for.

- Check the domain availability for names you are considering. It is a good idea to do this before you decide on a name so you can ensure the URL that matches your business name is available. You can go to any domain registrar, such as www.godaddy.com, to do this. As soon as you decide on a business name, purchase the accompanying URL. If you aren't quite certain of the name and you're vacillating between two or three options, you may want to buy the domain for all three. They are inexpensive and they get bought up easily. The more you go back and check on a name to see if it's still available, the higher the chance it will be purchased because analytics will show it as a highly searched name and there are companies that buy up such domains with the intent to sell them at heavily inflated prices.

- Conduct a business name search through your state's licensing department to make sure another company is not already licensed under that name. (In Washington state you will find this at www.dor.wa.gov. Use your favorite search engine to find your local licensing department.)

- Check the Secretary of State business listings as well; this is where LLCs and corporations are found. (The Secretary of state for Washington is located at www.sos.wa.gov. You can conduct a search to find your state's Secretary of State.)

- Verify if the name you desire is a registered trademark through the United States Patent and Trademark Office at www.uspto.gov. If you license your company under a name that is registered as a trademark, you can get yourself in a very sticky situation legally and you will have to immediately cease doing business under that name, which can have a detrimental impact on your business, sales, and expenses.

If you already have an established business name, you may consider the items above and determine whether your name is worth keeping or if you are better off changing the name. While this could cost you time and money now to make the transition, it may bring you more sales in the long run. A simple way to change your business name for better marketability is to add a DBA (doing business as) to your current license, rather than starting over with a completely new name and license. You will do this directly through your state's licensing department.

When I first started my business, I did so under the name Life Leaders International, Inc. A couple of years in, I realized this name did not accurately portray the message and vibe I wanted to create. I decided to change the business name to Accelerated Results 365 and completely rebranded the company. I kept the original name and added the new name to my license as a DBA. This was quick, simple, and inexpensive to do. After creating Accelerated Results 365, I became excited about my business. The result of the change was that I felt excited, energized, and confident in increasing my prices and my business began to take off. This is the power of having the right name.

Now I use Life Leaders International as my parent or umbrella company and as I take on new business ventures, I add a new branch to my business by adding another DBA. The publisher of this book, Gateway Inspirations, is one of the branches of Life Leaders International, Inc.

5. Purchase your personal domain name (URL).

Most people don't see this as part of the process of running a business. While this may not be critical for your type of business, it is recommended that you purchase the URL for your own name. Owning your personal name domain has many benefits including, but not limited to the following:

- If you do not buy it, someone else likely will and you want to be the one to own it.

- If someone else owns your name URL, you have no control over what is posted and what others will find when they do a search for your name.

- Owning your personal name domain has an impact on how you show up in Google and other search engines.

- You can choose to have a separate webpage sharing about you (and not your business) which can help prospective clients connect with you on a more personal level (thus developing trust and rapport) or you can set it up as a redirect to your business site so that when someone searches your name and clicks on your personal URL they will be sent directly to your business page.

I guarantee your name will be searched over the internet; some people will think of you by your business name and will search for you through your business, others will remember you by your personal name and will search for you using your personal name – give them multiple avenues in which they can find you!

6. **Choose the business structure that works best for you and obtain the appropriate licenses accordingly.**

There are multiple entity types to choose from, including sole-proprietor, partnership, LLC, S-Corporation and C-Corporation.

Carefully consider what type of entity you to choose. There are pros and cons to each. A sole proprietorship is most common for new businesses because it is the easiest form to establish, however, it is also the riskiest type. As a sole proprietor, you are responsible for any liabilities pertaining to the business. This means you are at risk of losing your personal assets in the event the business defaults on debts or ends up in a lawsuit.

An LLC and S-Corp are usually the best options because they give you the most protection of your personal assets by separating them from your business. There are different tax consequences and benefits of each. Reducing your tax obligation by incorporating is a great way to increase your profits.

It is important to also understand there are additional annual reporting requirements for a corporation; make sure you know what they are and how to file them. If you already have an established business that is not currently setup as an LLC or S-Corp, review the benefits and decide if it would be beneficial to change your business structure. Before you decide what is right for you, be sure to consult a reputable CPA and business attorney.

> Incorporating your business could be the biggest tax-saving strategy you will ever use.
>
> (Jacob M. Hanes, CPA and Founder, Action Tax Services, LLC)

Filing for a business license is simple and can be done online. If you plan to register as a sole proprietor or partnership, you will file directly with your state's department of licensing. If you intend to be an LLC or S-Corp, you will first apply with the Secretary of State of your choice. (No matter your state of residence, you can file your LLC or corporation in any state. Each state has varying fees and taxes. Be familiar with these before you choose which state to file in.) Once you have received your license from the Secretary of State, you will need to submit an application with the Department of Licensing in your state.

7. **Check for and obtain the proper permits.**

Some businesses, depending on the service or product you are offering, require special permits. Be sure to research if you will need one or more of these and what kinds are required. You can learn more about these requirements at www.sba.gov or your local state's department of licensing.

8. **Apply for an EIN – Employer Identification Number.**

This is a unique number assigned to your business by the IRS. For some businesses, this number is required, for others it's optional. You can find out if you need to apply for one at https://www.irs.gov/businesses/small-businesses-self-employed/do-you-need-a-new-ein.

Once you have gone through the preparation steps for starting or expanding your business, compile it into a simple written document. I have included a sample template on the next page. If the business plan is for your information only, this template will suffice. If you plan to obtain financing, you will need a more comprehensive plan. I recommend using the template by the Small Business Administration at www.sba.gov.

Your Business Name

Product/service offering:

Market need (why you offer this product/service, what makes it a good product/service to sell and how you know people will buy it – refer to your notes from the market analysis exercises):

Target market (demographics for who you will sell to – refer to your notes from the market analysis):

Type of entity and accompanying benefits (sole proprietorship, partnership, LLC, S-Corp, C-Corp):

Cost of doing business (list expected expenses):

Funding (explain how you will fund or finance operations):

Revenue (estimate your revenue for years one through five):

Marketing plan (how you will promote your product and find your buyers):

Building Exponential Profits
Tool # 3 – The Saw

There are many types of saws that may come in manual use or electric form. A saw is used to cut through material and transform it, giving it a different look, appeal, and often purpose. For example, a saw can be used to cut down a tree that is turned into firewood, used in processing paper, or becomes lumber for building.

Different saws are used for different purposes. Before deciding what saw is appropriate for a project, you would first decide on what you want to create – in other words, the end result.

When you are creating the plan for your business, look ahead and think about what you want to accomplish. What purpose do you want your business to fulfill? What is your objective? And formulate your goals and your plan around that.

Chapter
4

TRANSITIONING TO OWNERSHIP

If you were to go from being a renter to a homeowner, you wouldn't immediately evacuate from your current residence in order to move into a home that you don't yet own or haven't yet built, would you? This is what many people do when they want to become a business owner – they quit their job to grow their business before the business is fully established and generating revenue. Do not give up your day job just yet!

Follow these five tips to prepare for your transition:

1. **Start building your business while you continue working at your current job.**

   While this isn't always an option, it's a good idea to take some time to put your feet in and test the waters to make sure ownership is right for you and to also have an income stream while you build.

2. **Create your own security.**

   When you leave your job, you will be leaving behind a consistent paycheck and benefits such as vacation and sick pay, insurances such as medical, life and others, and retirement funds such as 401k, profit sharing and stock options. You can prepare yourself for the change by making sure you have an alternative cash flow, as was discussed in chapter three. Remember to be careful with the option you select, seek professional advice, and choose wisely.

3. **Share your thoughts on starting a business with others.**

A large part of growing a successful business is making sure others know you are in business and they are aware of what you offer. Even before you begin your business, it is a good idea to start talking about it and letting others know what you're going to be doing and what your vision is. This will generate interest, potential customers, and may spark new ideas you had not thought of yourself.

4. **Be careful of nay-sayers.**

There likely will be several well-meaning friends and family members who will try to stop you from starting a business or taking on new ventures in your current business. They will give you all the reasons why you shouldn't do so. Once you have decided that owning or expanding a business is right for you and you've properly prepared for ownership, stick to your plan and don't let them hold you back.

This is your dream and your life. It is up to you to build it and prove you can!

5. Make the Jump!

There comes a time when you've done all you can do to prepare and you may still find yourself having trepidation over the idea of leaving your current line of work – that's when it's time to make the jump. Fear is a great paralyzer; if you wait for there to be no fear, you will probably never get started. When you make the jump, you will find it is not as scary as it seems, and you will be glad you did.

Even after being in business for several years, you may find yourself reassessing your business plan, products, and processes. At times, you may need to make the jump all-over again in order to effectively grow.

Building Exponential Profits
Tool # 4 – The Measuring Tape

A builder uses a measuring tape many times throughout the process of building a home, from drawing the blueprint and finishing the sketches to making the final cut before assembling the materials.

Be sure to measure each step along your path in business ownership. From start-up to expansion, be clear you are making the right cuts – when to build, when to leave another profession, when to add on a new product or service, when and how to market, and so forth.

PHASE TWO

BUILD

A big business starts small.

Richard Branson

Chapter
5

ASSEMBLING YOUR CREW

Now that you have done the prep-work for starting or expanding your business, it is time to put together the crew to efficiently help you build it.

In building a house there are several professionals that become involved in the process such as an architect or general contractor to oversee the entire project from start to finish. This person acts as a project manager and works with a team of other specialized professionals who join during various stages of the process such as an electrician, drywaller, plumber, HVAC installer, and painter.

Likewise, regardless of what phase your business is in, it is important to have a team to guide you in profitably growing and maintaining it. Studies have shown that business owners who assemble this specialized crew attain greater profit margins and they are better prepared for and protected from problems that arise. Your key team players are the ones that will help protect your business and should consist of the following:

- Business consultant or coach - at Accelerated Results 365, we provide both coaching and consulting throughout each phase of building your business to guide you in developing and implementing your plan so you can exponentially grow your profits using the tools in this book as well as many others.

- Business attorney – it is not a matter of "if" you will need an attorney but rather "when", and the earlier the better (including at the beginning). Preparation and avoidance of a potential legal issue costs much less than what you'll pay if you are ever involved in a litigation, in both money and time. If you are on a tight budget, speak with an attorney to ensure you have at least the most important protections put in place.

> You can pay an attorney a relatively little now or you risk paying a lot more later. At a minimum, in addition to your organizational documents, make sure you have an attorney prepare these two critical documents to remain survivable - Terms & Conditions for your website, and basic separate agreements for your vendors and customers, though those likely will need to be modified, at least somewhat, for the particular situation/vendor/customer. (Note: Depending on your business, the Terms and Conditions for your website may cover your customers.)
>
> (Reputable Business Attorney)

- CPA – tax laws are constantly changing. It's hard enough to understand the 75,000 pages of tax code let alone keep up with the continuous revisions. You want to have someone on your team who specializes in these codes and stays apprised of the new laws, otherwise, you may receive an unwanted visit from "Uncle Sam".

> Having a great CPA is critical for the financial health of your business. Analyzing your financial data allows you to make important and substantive decisions, and a CPA is both an expert and ally during this process.
>
> (Steven Djordjevich, CPA Steven Djordjevich Certified Public Accountants and Business Advisors)

- Insurance agent or broker – having the proper business insurance coverages in place is important to protect against potential property damage or lawsuits against your company. Without it, you may find yourself paying costly expenses for repairs or legal issues.

- Financial advisor – it's a good idea to have someone who is skilled in understanding the market and making financial decisions to guide you in making wise decisions with your money, investments, and any debts you may take on.

As you decide who to bring on as part of your

crew, be sure you choose reputable experts who are highly skilled in their profession and have a proactive and growth mindset. Get to know them on a personal level to establish a high level of trust between you and them and so they know and understand the needs of your business.

Small business owners are lacking in some of the robust amenities of publicly traded organizations. One of the amenities that many businesses go without is a board of directors. The owner is responsible for everything, and so the thought of directors influencing the owner's actions, especially when needing to apply scarce dollars to directorships, can make any owner simply resign to the fact that there will be no board. That does not have to be the case if, as an owner, you are willing to invest some time in developing a relationship with what I term a virtual board. I think that you need at least four main players - the CPA, the money person, the lawyer, and the connector.

Your ability to connect with them, present your business challenges, and to ask their opinion and receive it is how they act as a board. You, as the owner, gather that information, process it, and then make the decisions in a more informed manner.

(Nicholas Fisher, Business Attorney, Law Offices of Nicholas Fisher)

Building Exponential Profits
Tool # 5 – The 5-in-1

A 5-in-1 tool is designed with multiple features to tackle several tasks with one tool. It is typically used by painters during prepping, painting, and cleanup. However, it can also be used for many other purposes such as a screwdriver, plaster chisel, scraper, can opener, and more.

The 5-in-1 represents your team that is comprised of a group of experts to oversee the key aspects of growing and protecting your business. These professionals will guide you in not only growing your business but also in protecting what you have worked so hard to build. You don't want to be without them!

Chapter
6

LAYING THE FOUNDATION

Since the publishing of my previous book "Overcoming Roadblocks to Success", the number one question I have been asked is, "What is the biggest roadblock business owners face?" While it's difficult to choose just one, as there are many and the struggles that come with running a business vary from person to person, there is one common obstacle that can hold back anyone from building a profitable business – you and the level of your mindset.

The three biggest excuses I hear people use for not excelling in business are lack of time, insufficient money, and inadequate education, training, or knowledge. As long as you focus on the absence of these resources, you will struggle. However, it is not the lack of these that is the true reason you will be held back; it's your belief around each of these areas that will. If you have a strong enough conviction around your ability to thrive despite any of these challenges, you will conquer every one of them!

Children are the best exemplars of this theory. Think of a time when you were young, and you wanted something badly. What did you do to get it?

I rented my first car when I was 16, before I even owned one. Some friends and I made plans to hang out on a Friday night, but there was one problem – none of us had a car. I had a driver's license but the only car my family owned was a big, maroon, stick-shift, station wagon – and I didn't know how to drive a manual vehicle at that time. But I was highly motivated! One of the friends involved was a boy I had a crush on the year before until he moved out of the area. He was in town for a visit, taller and cuter than before he left. I wanted to spend time with him so badly that I was determined to find a way to make it possible. I noticed a Toyota Corolla in the parking lot of the apartment complex where I lived that had a "For Sale" sign in the window. I knocked on the apartment door closest to where the car was parked and asked if the tenant was the owner. I made an offer to "rent" the car for the night for $30. Much to my amazement, to this very day, the owner agreed to my offer!

You and only you are responsible for your mindset. Unlike most anything else in your business, you cannot delegate it or hire someone else to manage it. You may pay a professional to teach you how to shift your mindset, but YOU are the one in charge.

You cannot build a house without a foundation.

And before you lay the foundation, you first need to make sure the land is surveyed, cleared, and leveled. Similarly, in business, you need to survey, clear and level your mind to prepare yourself for exponential growth.

Here are some ways you can create a powerful mindset that sets you up for success.

1. **Define what success means to you and how you will measure it.**

   Many people gauge their success by comparing themselves to others and how much money they make versus the other person, not considering their own circumstances and amount of growth.

   Success is also often quantified by how much money a person makes or the amount of revenue acquired by a company. But what is success really? It varies from person to person and it isn't necessarily about money.

   Here's a story to illustrate this point:

   > Jonathan grew up in a well-to-do family as an only child. Some would say he was raised with a "silver spoon" in his mouth. At the age of 25 he received an inheritance of $100,000 from his grandfather and he used it to start a tech-company. Within five years he was generating $1 million.

Rose, on the other hand, had very little growing up. Her single mother became ill and unable to work by the time she was fourteen. They lived on welfare, but it wasn't enough to pay rent and keep food on the table, so Rose took on cleaning jobs to help take care of her younger brother and sister. After high school, Rose worked her way through college while continuing to provide financial support for her mom and siblings. As the first person in her family to earn a degree, she graduated and was hired by a large retail store making minimum wage. Eventually, she worked her way up the ladder to CFO, making an annual income of $300,000.

Who would you consider to be more successful, Jonathan or Rose?

How do *you* define your success?

- By how much revenue you generate?

- By how high your profits are?

- By how many people you help?

- By how many products you sell?

- By how many people you recruit and train in a new skill?

- By how much time you spend with your family?

- By what others think about you?

The possible definitions are endless and only you can decide what makes you successful.

2. **Develop an internal environment conducive to success.**

Your internal environment is your thinking or your belief system which is the key to your success. If you spend most of your time with thoughts of negativity, you will continually struggle with progressing in your business and will likely give up. Negative thoughts such as doubt, frustration, and discouragement are natural, and we all have them at times. It is what you do with them that matters. You can either let them stick around and grow or you can clear your mind of them.

Here is an effective process for removing negativity from your mind:

- Become aware of negative thinking. Because most of our thinking is done at a subconscious level, we often don't realize when we are having negative thoughts. Pay attention to what goes through your mind, especially during stressful and uncomfortable situations. Do you find yourself thinking things like "I'm not good enough", "it's too hard", "I can't do this", or "I should be doing (fill in the blank)"? These are what I call "closed opportunity phrases" because when we allow such ideas to remain, we become closed off to recognizing the many wonderful opportunities around us and our growth becomes stifled.

- Reframe your thoughts. Many people think ridding your mind of negativity is like taking out the trash – you can just throw it away or let it go to never be seen again. Do you remember a time when you were bothered by a situation and someone told you to "just let it go"? How well did that work? Usually, it doesn't. Often, when we try to "let it go" it gets worse because we *actually* spend more time ruminating on how to let it go so our focus remains on the one thing we don't want to think about.

The most effective way to rid your thoughts of something you don't want is to "reframe" the thought. For example, when words enter your mind such as, "I can't grow my business because people don't want to spend money," you can reframe it to "In order for my business to be successful, I can show people how using my services will help them make more money."

- Feed your mind good food. What you put into your mind impacts how you think. There is a lot of negativity in the world around us that we don't have control over, but we do have control over what we focus on. Use your time wisely on filling your mind with positive things such as uplifting books, podcasts, and music and limit the amount of time you spend on social media and watching the news. You will notice your thoughts become more empowering and your awareness of opportunities will be heightened.

- Feed your body good food. The foods you eat have an impact on your mood and your mindset. Limit your sugar and fat intake and fuel your body with foods high in vitamins and minerals; you will be able to focus better, think more clearly, and make wiser decisions for accelerating your growth and increasing your profits.

> There is a strong correlation between your eating habits and your productivity. What you choose to put in your mouth will improve or challenge both your physical and mental health. Your nutrition strategy should be as important as your business strategy.
>
> (Celine Brozovich, Founder, Baykenji Health

- Practice daily gratitude. It is easy to sink into a downward spiral of everything we don't have and want. When we focus on what we don't have, we breed negativity. On the other hand, when we choose to put our attention into the things we DO have, we create positivity. And studies show the more we focus on what we have, the more we will obtain.

- Recognize and acknowledge daily wins. As a society, we focus more on what we didn't accomplish than we do on what we DID accomplish. Let's pretend you had a goal to lose 20 pounds and get in shape this year. You implement new habits of working out and eating healthier. After four weeks, you find you didn't lose any weight. How does it feel to realize your weight has not changed? Most people get discouraged by this and go back to their old habits and never reach their desired weight. If you look at what you did accomplish rather than what you didn't, you may notice that you have more energy, your waistline is a bit smaller, you have the strength to carry more, and you're more productive. When you recognize these accomplishments, you will feel successful and be motivated to continue your path to a healthier lifestyle.

- Implement regular movement. Moving our body releases chemicals in our brain that gives us energy, helps us think clearly, and makes us happier. Having a routine for regular exercise and incorporating movement throughout the day is important for your physical health as well as your mental health. Regularly schedule time for exercise and whenever possible, get up and walk around, stand instead of sit, and stretch your body.

- Practice daily spirituality. Whether you prefer prayer or meditation, be sure to take time each day in spiritual contemplation. Such practice will help you stay focused and strong during challenges.

3. **Design an encouraging external environment.**

Your external environment includes everything

that surrounds you – what you have on your walls, the organization and cleanliness of the areas where you spend your time, and the people you associate with. Do these things create a sense of peace or stress? Are the people you're with encouraging or discouraging? What can you change in your environment to invoke greater inspiration?

4. Serve others.

When we serve others, something magical happens – we are blessed. We feel good about ourselves which builds confidence and improves our belief system. When we are doing something for someone else, it disrupts our negative thinking because it takes our mind off our own problems and our challenges tend to feel smaller. Additionally, when we do good for others, others want to help us in return. Sometimes it comes back to us from those we have helped and other times it comes back through the support of someone else. Others become our advocates that contribute to the growth of our business.

5. Make your bed every morning.

Studies have shown that making your bed leads to greater success because it sets the tone for the rest of the day; it's easy to do and a simple way to start your day with having accomplished something. This simple accomplishment leads to greater achievement.

6. Get up when your alarm goes off – don't hit the snooze button.

How you respond to your alarm also sets the tone for the day. Your alertness and productivity increase when you get up when your alarm goes off. Hitting snooze decreases your productivity throughout the day and you will find yourself feeling more sluggish.

7. Get sufficient sleep.

How much quality sleep you get has a huge impact on your productivity and ability to think clearly. When you are tired, you are more likely to make costly mistakes which can be very detrimental to your overall profits.

8. Take cold showers.

Like most people I recommend this to, you may be thinking there is no way you are going to do this one. You're probably thinking I'm crazy and wondering what cold showers have to do with building exponential profits. I used to think taking cold showers was absurd, until I met Brent Friedman, Hollywood Writer and Producer. He told me one of the keys to his success was that he takes cold showers. I admitted to him that I know of many successful people that I admire, such as Tony Robbins, who make a similar claim, but I didn't think it was necessary for success. He called me out and asked if I believed Tony. He challenged me to give it a try for 14 days. My competitive side kicked in and I replied, "I'll do 30!" The next day when I woke, I wondered why I had made such a commitment and dreaded getting out of bed. I have been taking cold showers since (most days). I really notice a difference between the days that I do and those that I don't. Cold showers are refreshing and energizing. They help with clarity in thinking and it's another way to start my day feeling accomplished; it is a great reminder that I can do difficult and uncomfortable things. And there are also many health benefits to taking cold showers.

Cold showers accomplish two important things: 1) the bracing water will increase circulation to help wake you naturally without caffeine or sugar; 2) the cold will always be uncomfortable, at least at first, which forces you to choose discomfort.

The second point is key because it's your daily reminder that discomfort is good for your body and your mind. Making one difficult decision to start your day is a great way to prepare yourself for whatever challenges lie ahead. If you can handle ice cold water at 7:00 in the morning, you can handle just about anything!

(Brent Friedman, Hollywood Writer & Producer)

9. **Acknowledge your small successes and be kind to yourself.**

Too often, people feel they need to accomplish something big before they celebrate a success. It's the little accomplishments along the way that add up to the big wins. When you take a moment to stop and recognize the small things, you can better keep the momentum going to stay motivated and do more. Additionally, by allowing yourself to take a break and be kind to yourself, you give yourself a chance to reboot and build energy to do greater things.

Building Exponential Profits
Tool # 6 – The Level

When laying the foundation of a house, if you don't make sure the foundation is level, you will end up with many structural issues in your home that will drastically hinder the ability to efficiently build and the life of the house will shortened.

Running a business often feels like riding a roller coaster. There are many obstacles that crop up along the way that will derail you and lead to the destruction of the business if you have not taken the time to create a clear and level mind. How you react to the challenges you face along the journey will define the sustainability of the business through your ability to adjust, adapt, pivot and remain profitable.

Chapter
7

CONSTRUCTING THE WALLS

Once you complete all the prep-work and the foundation is ready, it gets exciting because things really start to come together as you begin constructing the walls – these are the things you do in your business to ensure it runs smoothly and is ready for growth. These are also several things that many business owners skip over.

1. **Do not mingle business transactions with your personal finances.**

   Open a bank account specifically for the business, separate from all personal accounts. If you mix business and personal and ever get audited by the IRS, you could find yourself with a big dilemma of paying extra taxes as well as heavy fines.

2. **Set up a financial tracking system.**

   If you already have a system in place, review it and determine its ease of use and effectiveness. Is it properly meeting your needs?

   Decide whether to do your own bookkeeping or hire a bookkeeper. This is a responsibility many business owners take on themselves without any experience.

If you aren't experienced with managing books and you are spending time on learning how to do it yourself, you are probably wasting time that could be spent on doing revenue generating activities.

If you decide to hire a bookkeeper, make sure you find a reputable one with experience and an understanding of how to prepare the books appropriately to easily pass on to your CPA at tax time. Most CPAs love it when the books are organized well because it saves them from wasting time on the little things so they can put their focus on the activities that bring in higher dollars for them.

3. **Become familiar with the various financial reports.**

The Income Statement (often referred to as the Profit and Loss Report or P&L), Balance sheet, and Cash Flow Statement are your three main reports. Even if you are using a bookkeeper, you need to be familiar with these and what they represent so that you have a handle on your financials and the health of your company. This will also help protect you from fraud. While you may know your bookkeeper personally and have full trust in him/her, you should never put 100% trust in anyone handling your money. It's just good business sense.

4. **Have an IT expert analyze your computer and other technology systems to ensure electronic security.**

   More and more we are bombarded with viruses that destroy our work and hackers that steal our private information.

   If you do not have the proper precautions in place to protect your data, not only are you putting your business at risk, but also your customers.

5. **Utilize a planning system.**

   I've worked with many business owners that weren't accustomed to or in the habit of using a planner and they lost a lot of time trying to manage and remember everything. Because they were unorganized with their time, they missed several opportunities for increasing their revenues.

6. **Implement a CRM (customer retention management) system.**

   Companies lose a lot of potential clients due to lack of following up with prospects. A CRM is a great way to keep track of leads and clients and when and how you have contact with them. It's also a good way to plan and schedule into your calendar your follow up with each prospect.

With consistent follow up, many of them will eventually become clients.

Having proper organizational structures in place will better position you for growth. If you grow before being prepared, you are more likely to fail.

Building Exponential Profits
Tool # 7 – The Hammer

Whether you use a handheld hammer or an electric nail gun, you need the proper tool for nailing together the frame and putting up the walls in order to finish the construction of your home.

To finish the building of your business, you need to nail together the final pieces that will allow your business to run smoothly and profitably. These consist of the systems you put in place to ensure efficiency. These systems help you free up your time for focusing on revenue generating activities.

PHASE THREE

DESIGN

Be so good they can't ignore you.

Steve Martin

Chapter
8

DESIGNING THE INTERIOR

When you get to the interior designing of a house, it's time to pick out the wall colors, furniture and fixtures. Within your business, this is the moment you get to design the look and feel of your business and prepare it for marketing. This is what we call your branding. Most businesses jump right to marketing before having their branding in place and struggle with getting sales because their message is not clear.

Many people don't understand what branding really is. When I say the word "brand" most think of the visual attributes that make up the logo, such as design and the color scheme. Your brand is more than just your logo.

> The key is to whet a potential customer's appetite with a juicy, engaging message that makes people sit up, care, and buy your brand.
>
> (Gerry Foster, Creator of The Big Brand Formula, Gerry Foster Branding)

The following steps will help you in developing your brand.

1. **Define and put into writing your mission and vision statements.**

   The purpose of your mission and vision statements is to give you, as the business owner, a clear direction for your business and to attract and connect your audience (referred to as your target market) to your company.

   Both statements are a critical piece in building a successful and thriving business. I recommend you have one of each for you personally as well as for your business.

   The business mission and vision can be shared with your prospective customers and included on your website and other marketing materials.

   Your personal mission and vision are about your life purpose and why you chose the business you did. This is something that is not shared with your customers.

   In developing your personal mission statement, you will define your "why" as in why you are in business and why you chose this career path. It will act as a beginning point for establishing your goals, defining your values, and ensuring your core values, personal goals, and business goals are in alignment. Having clarity with your mission will help you in the decision making throughout the various areas of your business such as with finance and budgeting, time management, marketing, target audience, etc.

Individuals and businesses who have a clearly defined and written vision are found to reach greater successes in a shorter time frame. Having a vision of where you want your business to go and what the specific desired outcomes and aspirations for your business and your personal life will help you progress toward those desired outcomes.

When you create your vision and consistently focus on the outcomes, you will be driven to find the "how" to accomplish those things.

Together, your business mission and vision statements should draw in your customers and in a clear and concise manner tell them how you are going to solve their problem, why you are the best person for doing so, and the impact you will make over the long-term.

2. Define specific and written goals.

Once you have developed your mission and vision, review your goals and refine them. Goal setting is a critical component of a successful business; they give you the direction in which you are taking your business and define the steps to get there.

3. **Update your business plan**.

   Your business plan will tie together your mission, vision and goals and help you stay focused on the things that will build your business.

4. **Design your logo.**

   Your logo is the visual representation of your company and what it has to offer. You want it to be high-quality, attractive, and memorable. Be sure that you use consistency with your logo and your color scheme for all marketing, both online and offline.

   There are many options available for designing your logo. You can do it yourself, do it online for cheap, hire a freelancer, or hire a professional designer.

   I recommend working with a professional designer to come up with something of high quality that truly represents your company and attracts the clients you desire.

   If you go with one of these other options, you risk damaging your company's reputation and you are more likely to revise your logo down the road, creating a greater expense because you'll need to redo your website, business cards, and all your print material.

5. Be a "walking billboard".

YOU are part of your company brand through your personal attributes, characteristics, values, and by how you represent yourself. Everywhere you go, you display a part of your brand so think of yourself as a "walking billboard" for your business and be aware of the message you put out into the world.

6. Get a current and professional headshot.

You will use your headshot throughout several aspects of your business including on your website and possibly your business cards. Many business owners make the mistake of using a headshot that is several years old and does not look like them anymore. This may confuse your customers and is not a good business practice. It is best to use a photo that is less than two years old.

Building Exponential Profits
Tool # 8 – The Paint Roller

In the building of your house, the paint brush represents the final touches – choosing the texture pattern and color of paint for the walls. As you do so, you will consider the purpose of each room, the furniture and décor you plan to use, and who will be invited in. You will then select the right type and color of paint and the appropriate paint roller and cover to create the message you want to portray and the feeling you desire to invoke within anyone entering that particular room. How you design a bedroom is going to differ from the way in which you design a room for entertaining.

The development and revising of your branding are similar to the process of choosing your wall texture, paint colors, and roller. The look and feel that you emanate through your branding is going to appeal to a particular type of person and you want to ensure it's the kind who you want to attract as a client.

Chapter
9

PLANNING THE HOUSEWARMING PARTY

Once you have your house complete and the interior design is finished, the next thing you will be excited to do is to show it off to all your friends. That's when it's time to begin planning a housewarming party.

In business, you want to show off your beautiful branding and the products you offer to your prospective clients; this is done through marketing.

These are some things you can do for bringing in customers to buy your services:

1. **Create an attractive website that accurately and clearly represents what you sell.**

   The purpose of your website it to provide quick information, build instant credibility, entice new customers, and provide a means for prospective and current customers to contact you for more information. Things to pay attention to when creating your website are:

   - Is it appealing and attractive?

   - Does it showcase a level of professionalism that is appropriate for your industry?

- Is your message clear and concise?

- Is it free of typos?

- Does it differentiate you from your competition and showcase you as the best in your industry?

2. **Prepare a written marketing plan.**

Having a marketing plan will help you best utilize your time and financial resources. You may find that some marketing strategies you try are ineffective. This is normal and in the early stages it makes sense to try various options and find what works best for you. Working with a professional may help guide you in quickly selecting the best avenues for you and make better use of how you spend your marketing dollars.

3. **Map out your sales funnel.**

Planning out your sales funnel will be a part of your marketing plan. For this piece, you will include the sales process in which you will capture and maintain your clients. You will define the starting point in how you market to your clients, how you pique their interest, how you capture their contact information, and what the next steps are for keeping them engaged (whether they buy or don't buy) so that you remain at the top of their mind as the best company to meet their needs.

4. Utilize social media marketing.

If you are not utilizing social media marketing as an avenue for your business, you may be missing out on important opportunities to build your customer base. Even if you don't have a business that typically draws clients through social media, it's still a good idea to have a presence because so many people use social media as a means to verify a business is legit and credible.

5. Take advantage of relationship marketing.

Relationship marketing is a low cost, and often free, way of promoting your services. Always be making connections and building relationships everywhere you go. You can do this through networking groups, chamber events, and speaking with friends and family. Be sure that you maintain a strategy for consistent follow up and keep your pipeline filled.

> Relationship marketing is the most important marketing tool you will use because people are more likely to do business with someone they connect with on a personal level.

6. Always be ready to give an elevator pitch.

This is often your first introduction to your business upon meeting someone new. You have a brief opportunity to make a first impression – make it a great and memorable one!

Create an elevator pitch that is unique, catchy, and short enough you could say it in 60 seconds or less (the time it would take to ride an elevator down one floor). You do not need to get into detail about what you do. Say "just enough" to pique interest.

Building Exponential Profits
Tool # 9 – The Ladder

A ladder is necessary for reaching places you can't reach on your own. It's used frequently not only during the construction of a home but also for maintaining it to prevent damage and keep the home looking beautiful. There are many different styles and sizes of ladders ranging in cost to fit various needs.

In your business, the ladder represents the ability to expand your reach to prospective customers who will learn of you and your company through marketing. Be sure to choose the right ladder, or marketing avenue, that gives you the best exposure to the right clients and provides a good ROI (return on investment – the benefit you get back verses the money you spend).

PHASE FOUR

EXPAND

Strength and growth come only through
continuous effort and struggle.

Napoleon Hill

Chapter
10

THE EXPONENTIAL FORMULA

When you decide your home no longer serves your needs and you want something bigger, you will either sell your home and upgrade to a larger place or you will expand the home you already have.

When you reach the point in your business when you are well established and running smoothly, you are ready to explode your growth. Many business owners try to grow too soon, too fast and their business implodes because they were not properly prepared for the growth. If you skipped over the preceding chapters because you've already been in business for several years and you felt you were beyond those phases, please go back and review them to make sure you have built a good, solid foundation for your business.

Sometimes expanding is simply adding on to what you are already doing, and sometimes you need to "knock down walls" to purge the pieces that no longer work and make the necessary updates.

Doing the following can help you expand your business and exponentially grow your profits.

1. **Hire a business consultant.**

   A consultant will look at your current processes and guide you in finding ways to maximize your time, effort, and money. At Accelerated Results 365, we conduct a P.O.W.E.R.R.™ analysis of the four core areas of your business (money, marketing, mindset, and movement), prepare a Report of Findings and Recommendations, and create a plan for implementing strategies for expansion and growing your profits.

2. **Analyze your revenue and expenses and find ways to increase your profit margin.**

   Look for things you are spending money on that you no longer need and can cut back on as well as those you can eliminate. Be careful in doing this – many business owners make cutbacks in some of the key areas that help their business grow and rather than achieving increased profits, they create declining profits. Your consultant can work together with you and your accountant to determine which reductions are beneficial and which ones are detrimental.

3. **Add a new product or service.**

   Review the needs of your customers and look for ways you can fulfill a need by adding new features to what you sell and offering a new product or service. Take into consideration the supply and demand of the current economy.

4. Improve your skills and learn new ones.

We previously covered the importance of investing in yourself and your business. If you want to exponentially grow your profits, you must always be improving yourself and your business processes. Never stop learning. Think of skills you can improve such as speaking, selling, negotiating, and communicating with your team and your clients.

5. Revise your brand.

People change and so do their interests, needs and desires. Many of the top successful companies, including Apple, Inc. understand the need to evolve their branding. They have changed their logo numerous times to adapt to the market to keep their customers interested while attracting new customers.

6. Get out of your comfort zone.

It's easy to become comfortable and complacent in your business and day-to-day tasks. Keep things fresh by constantly pushing yourself out of your comfort zone.

7. Develop an abundance mindset.

Many owners reach a revenue level they're comfortable with once they have enough to cover all the bills and pay themselves an income sufficient for covering their personal expenses and they stop working toward growth. Once you stop thinking about growth, the business will begin to wane. Think abundantly. What can you do with the money when you double, triple, or quadruple your profits? Do you have a charity you're passionate about? What lives can you change?

8. Empower your employees.

Your employees will reach a point when their job duties seem mundane and their productivity plateaus. Companies often don't see this happen until they notice a drop in sales. You can empower your employees by making small changes to their responsibilities or challenging them with something new. Give them opportunities to be a leader. Acknowledge their accomplishments (small and big) and be specific when thanking them. And offer incentives. Having in place benefits such as medical insurance and a 401k help to retain employees but it's not sufficient for keeping them engaged. Implementing a recognition system such as a monthly "best team player" builds engagement and keeps productivity up.

9. **Boost your appearance**.

   How do you dress and present yourself? Is it
   appropriate for your market? Remember, you
   are a walking billboard and the most important
   piece of your marketing. How you present
   yourself is going to attract or detract clients
   and make a difference in the type you do
   attract.

10. **Increase your involvement and presence in
    your community.**

   An excellent way to grow your profits is by
   getting out in your community to connect
   with new prospective customers. In doing
   this, be sincere and participate in ways you
   truly resonate with. If your intentions are
   fake or simply to just make money, others
   will sense it, and that may be more damaging
   to your business.

The Exponential Equation

Do you remember the good ol' days of high school and sitting in algebra class listening to the teacher drone on about the value of "x"? You may have thought you were never going to use this stuff in "real life". If you had not already found a use for algebra, you have now.

The exponential equation states $y=ab^x$. What this shows is that growing your profits exponentially requires that you combine and multiply various factors (the activities in your business as addressed above), then multiply them to the exponential power of "x". As a business owner, this equation indicates what you need to do to build your profits exponentially – multiply your activity and efforts exponentially!

Building Exponential Profits
Tool # 10 – The Sledgehammer

A sledgehammer is often used for the destruction of something such as a building. It is built with a long handle and a heavy metal head, designed to build momentum when it's swung in order to add force when it strikes the object it's being used on.

When you want to explode your business and generate exponential profits, you will need to de-struct certain aspects and processes in order to implement and build new, efficient ones. And you want to do so with force (your commitment and willingness to change) and momentum (the speed at which you act).

BONUS

Keep Calm and Carry On

World War II Poster

THE UNEXPECTED STORM

You can build your house and put in place all the right and necessary protections, but you may not be prepared for every storm that comes. What do you do if a lightning and thunderstorm rolls in, accompanied by large hale balls? Or a tornado comes through and destroys your home?

This is what the year 2020 felt like for many businesses when the COVID-19 pandemic spread throughout the world, creating a recession like none ever experienced by those living at the time. It was unexpected and caused great fear and uncertainty in both business owners and consumers and over 100,000 American small businesses permanently closed.[3]

What do you do in a time like this to protect your business?

1. **Make decisions wisely.**

   It's during moments of fear and uncertainty that you're more likely to make poor decisions that could hurt your business for good, such as terminating key employees who have the skills necessary to innovatively keep the business running, or cutting out marketing which keeps the business noticed and at top of mind for your customers. If you ARE able to recover, it's likely to be a long, hard road.

2. Act fast and pivot.

Reassess your product or service and determine if it still meets the needs of the current market. If not, determine what you can do to modify or completely change what you offer to meet the needs of the current economy. Analyze several possible options, make a decision, and move forward quickly.

This is exactly what Canlis, a high-end, fine dining restaurant in Seattle, Washington did. They recognized that "fine dining is not what Seattle needs right now." While many other restaurants were shutting down, the owners of Canlis quickly pivoted to simple, boxed meals available for pick-up or delivery - and livestreaming smooth piano music into the homes of their customers as well as hosting Bingo for a family night of fun in order to safely provide jobs for employees while continuing to serve the community. [4]

3. Continue marketing your products and services.

Businesses tend to cut back and often eliminate their marketing budget during a financial crisis when in fact, this is one of the most critical times you need to be marketing in order to stay in front of your prospective clients. This is a good time to reassess your marketing budget and avenues to ensure the best return for your money spent.

4. Continue working with a coach or consultant.

This is another area where companies tend to cut back and avoid spending money yet having a professional help you navigate the challenges can be the very thing that keeps the business running.

> Like everyone else, I too, was impacted by the great pandemic. I decided to use this time as an opportunity to better position my business to stand out in the industry. I hired a branding expert to help me boost my messaging, a new coach to keep me grounded and focused on the most important activities for building my business, and I increased my marketing. While other businesses were closing, mine was growing.

Curveball, a LAF Tech signature improv exercise, is a great and fun way to build resiliency, team collaboration, and confidence.

The entire point of the exercise is to get everyone talking with the side benefits being that everyone also sits bolt-upright, their heartbeats accelerate, and their brains release both endorphins and dopamine because no one wants to be called on!

Each person gets a word to start with, and their immediate challenge is to "just start talking about it." The goal is to create a funny story on the fly! Then the "audience," when prompted by a leader, tosses out a new word every 20-30 seconds. This exercise can be used to start a meeting off with high energy to build synergy and engagement.

(Marcelle Allen & Brian Trendler, LAF Tech Founders)

Building Exponential Profits
Tool # 11 – The Shovel

There are many types of storms that can come through and cause havoc on your home, tearing it to pieces. You will need a shovel to clear the broken remnants and rebuild what was damaged.

When a terrible crisis hits your business, be prepared to clean up the mess and rebuild. You may be able to build it back to what it used to be; and you may have to build it differently. Be willing to do whatever is needed to keep your business running. You can overcome the storm. And when you do, your business will be better than it was before the storm.

EPILOG

THINK BIG AND TAKE RISKS

I am a big advocate of thinking big and I encourage and push all my clients to do so. Even if you don't fully reach a goal, when you expand your thinking and reach for bigger ones than what you believe you can do, you're going to reach further than when you set goals that you believe are achievable.

> Catherine is the product of her program and it makes what she shares more genuine.
>
> (Casey Davis, Executive Director, Edmonds Food Bank)

I was contacted about four months prior to the writing of this book by T.C. Bradley, T.V. show host of God Made Millionaire, for an opportunity to appear on his show. I felt the show was out of my league, but I accepted the offer and chose to use it to push myself into something bigger than what I was currently doing.

I opted for an interview slot the furthest out that I was offered with the intention that I would have a new book written, edited, and published by the time the show aired so I would have something tangible to promote my business.

While four months seemed an unreasonable amount of time to give myself to write a book, especially as a busy, single-mom, I chose to challenge myself because when I publicly commit to something, I work hard to make it happen.

I set out to write my book and I nearly gave up. I had a topic and title picked out and I began but I didn't make it very far before I hit "writer's block". Weeks went by with my schedule filling up with other commitments and I decided I was losing too much time to write the book. It didn't seem like a good idea anymore to write a book and I decided I would find a different way to present my business on the show.

Meanwhile, a friend of mine who runs a business as a General Contractor invited me on a couple of cleaning and remodeling jobs since I was home with less work and more time on my hands due to a lockdown order implemented by local government officials in response to the COVID-19 pandemic. While I'm very experienced and thorough when it comes to cleaning, I had never done any kind of house remodeling. I had plenty of projects waiting to be done on my own home, but I was afraid to do so much as pick up a brush and paint a wall in fear that I would completely mess up something.

One opportunity led to another and then another and I was soon introduced to the Balogh family who I quickly became friends with. I spent the following months helping them with a full remodel of a home they had recently purchased. Through my experience with various construction projects, primarily with the Baloghs, I learned how to lay down vapor barriers in crawl spaces, insulate attics and walls, install heat ducting, hang drywall, texture and paint walls, and so much more.

I found that I enjoyed the contract work because it was mentally rewarding to learn new skills and it kept me physically active while the gyms were closed and the weather wasn't optimal for outside running. I remained very busy as I continued to engage in activities to grow my business while juggling my side jobs.

As the time for me to leave for my T.V. interview neared, I began to regret that I hadn't written a book.

Then two weeks before I was to travel for my interview, a strong feeling hit me that I needed to write. The idea seemed crazy, even more so than when I thought of doing it three and a half months earlier. However, I listened to the prompting and committed to writing. Soon everything came together at an accelerated rate; I quickly came up with a title and had the cover designed before I even began writing. By the time I flew out of town, the manuscript was nearly 50% complete. The first draft of my manuscript was finished within four weeks.

During the following weeks of editing and revising my book, something magical happened and my business began to take off.

A key to building exponential profits is to challenge yourself by setting big goals; the bigger the goal, the bigger the profits will be that follow.

Exponential growth is not going to happen overnight – it will happen over time with patience and persistence.

ABOUT THE AUTHOR

Catherine M. White founded Accelerated Results 365 to assist businesses in achieving exponential growth and developing powerful, productive teams.

Having come from a family of eight children, financial resources were sparse growing up, so Catherine learned by the early age of ten that it was up to her to take charge of her life by earning her own income. As an older sister, she gained many skills such as nurturing, teaching, and managing time, people and money which she was able to apply to her first careers in house cleaning, babysitting, and delivering newspapers at the wee hours of the morning before leaving for school, walking uphill in the snow (no joke!).

With a love for math, helping people, and being independent, Catherine knew by the time she went to college that she wanted to start her own business, so she decided to obtain a degree in accounting.

Life took her down a challenging journey as a single parent of four young children yet she remained focused on her dream and continued to educate herself in the various aspects of business while raising her family, working multiple jobs, and pursuing various business opportunities.

With over twenty years of experience in leading

individuals and teams to innovative, successful outcomes, Catherine uses her financial, managerial, HR, and accounting expertise to support businesses in developing practical and efficient processes while building definable goals that align the organization with its teams and customers through her proprietary program, P.O.W.E.R.R.™

ABOUT ACCELERATED RESULTS 365

Our Mission: To build sustainable businesses and self-reliant individuals, increasing your team's productivity, and exponentially growing your revenue.

Our Vision: To create cultures in businesses that leave a mark on the world!

Accelerated Results 365 is the only consulting firm that utilizes the innovative, proven, six-step P.O.W.E.R.R.™ system for small to medium-sized businesses who want to leave a mark on the world by improving their employees' lives and influencing communities in a time when companies are looking for ways to have a greater impact and expand their growth with integrity while increasing their profits with acceleration and ease.

Statistics show that working with a coach or consultant will help you grow a thriving business at an accelerated rate. There are many systems available that promise quick growth, yet many of these systems are not sustainable. At Accelerated Results 365, we will guide you through a process for creating quick AND sustainable growth.

P.O.W.E.R.™

Possibilities • Outcome • Workable Steps • Empowering Environment • Resources • Rewards

Possibilities: Gain clarity by setting goals that stretch you and define your vision and mission, so you stand out among your competition.

Most business owners lack clarity in where their business is headed and how they will get there. In this step you will explore what is possible stretching beyond your current thinking into a bigger vision while aligning your team with the organizational goals, thus generating natural buy-in.

Outcome: Develop a vision of the outcome of your success by engaging all the senses – touch, see, hear, smell, taste, emotions.

In order to know how to get to where you're going, you need to know what you're aiming for; In this step you will remove confusion, build innovation, and boost motivation.

Workable Steps: Create an action plan by breaking your big goals into micro steps.

Without an action plan, there is a lack of direction and a great feeling of overwhelm and overload. In this step you will reduce overwhelm and stress and increase successful completion of your goals.

Empowering Environment: Identify your current internal and external environment and create an environment for success.

A non-empowering environment becomes toxic; toxicity spreads through the team, to the customers and into the community and destroys the organization's credibility. In this step you will increases sales through greater exposure within the community.

Resources: Explore resources, processes, and opportunities by thinking-out-of-the-box to expand your network, market your service, and generate leads that turn to clients.

Many people are closed or narrow-minded and become stagnant - keeping an open mind and being able to continually look for a solution is critical for growth in any market and economy. In this step you will build organizational innovation and increase possibilities for expansive growth.

Rewards: Define a system for acknowledging and rewarding the big and small successes of yourself and your team.

People want to be noticed and recognized but most do not take the time to recognize their own accomplishments. In this step you will ignite momentum, build energy, and increase motivation which leads to reaching **massive** results!

ARE YOU READY TO BUILD
EXPONENTIAL PROFITS?!

Check out our free resources at
www.beyondbreakingeven.com/resources

Call or email today
for your free consultation!

catherine@acceleratedresults365.com
www.acceleratedresults365.com
(206) 422-4450

REFERENCES

1. Tobak, Steve. "Lies, Damn Lies and Statistics About Entrepreneurs." *Entrepreneur*, Entrepreneur, 23 Oct. 2014, www.entrepreneur.com/article/238800#:~:text=Crunching%20U.S.%20Census%20and%20survey,another%2030%20percent%20lose%20money.

2. SBA, Office of Advocacy. "Frequently Asked Questions, Advocacy: the Voice of Small Business in Government." *Small Business Association*, Sept. 2012, www.sba.gov/sites/default/files/FAQ_Sept_2012.pdf.

3. Long, Heather. "Small Business Used to Define America's Economy. The Pandemic Could Change That Forever." *Washington Post*, Washington Post, 12 Mar. 2020, www.washingtonpost.com/business/2020/05/12/small-business-used-define-americas-economy-pandemic-could-end-that-forever/.

4. Guarente, Gabe. "Fine Dining Icon Canlis Turns to Takeout, Drive-Thru, and Delivery During COVID-19 Outbreak." *Eater Seattle*, Eater Seattle, 12 Mar. 2020, https://seattle.eater.com/2020/3/12/211 77204/canlis-closes-main-dining-room-opens-three-casual-restaurants.

Made in the USA
Columbia, SC
21 June 2024